SUMMER
SPORTS SAFETY

by Carol Barkin
illustrated by Doris Ettlinger

**McGraw-Hill
School Division**

New York   Farmington

Summer! It's a time for fun and for playing sports. When the weather gets warm, you and your friends probably wheel out your bikes or put on your in-line skates. You might spend time at a pool, a lake, or even the ocean shore. Perhaps you go for hikes in the woods. Maybe you play tennis with a friend or shoot hoops in the playground.

If you join team sports, there's usually a coach. Coaches help players improve their skills. They also try to make sure that players don't get hurt. If you don't have your own coach, you can still make the right choices to help keep yourself safe.

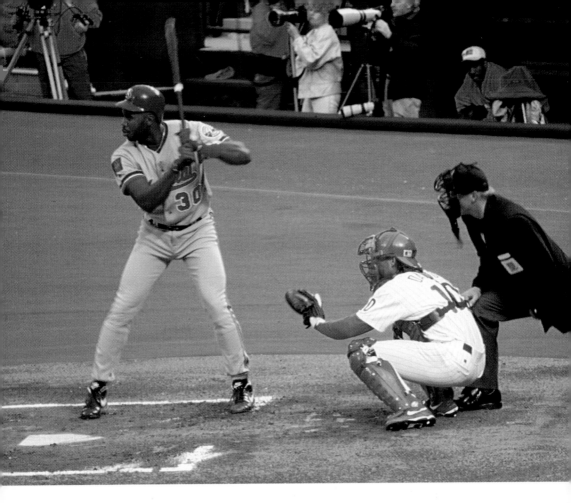

Accidents can keep you from playing your favorite summer sport. That's not much fun! If you follow a few simple safety rules, you can enjoy sports all summer long.

Safety in summer sports can be described in one word: protection. Why do soccer players wear shin pads? To protect their bones, joints, and muscles from being injured. What about the mask worn by baseball catchers? It protects their faces from being hit by a baseball. You can probably think of a lot of other ways that professional athletes protect themselves while they play.

You also need protection when you play summer sports. There are a lot of things you can do. Although these things are not hard to do, you have to *remember* to do them. Still, protecting yourself makes you feel better and play better, too.

What's the first thing you think of when someone mentions summer? It's probably the hot weather. The Sun's heat may feel great, but it can cause sunburn. Sunburn hurts! A bad sunburn can make you feel sick, give you a terrible headache, and even cause blisters. Even a light burn or pale tan can lead to skin damage.

However, it's easy to avoid too much exposure to the Sun. Here are some ways to protect your skin.

1. Use sunscreen or sunblock of at least SPF 15 on uncovered skin. Don't forget the tops of your ears, the back of your neck, and the tops of your feet.
2. Wear a hat with a visor or brim to protect your face.
3. Remember that sunscreen is not completely waterproof, so slather on more after a swim.
4. Get out of the Sun if you start to turn pink or visibly tan, or if your skin feels too hot.

Hot weather and physical activity make people sweat a lot. That's good! Sweating keeps your body from overheating. However, it also means you lose more water than you usually do.

One way to protect your body in the summer is to drink a lot of water. A rule of thumb is to drink six to eight glasses of water every day, all year round. This replaces the water you lose when you sweat.

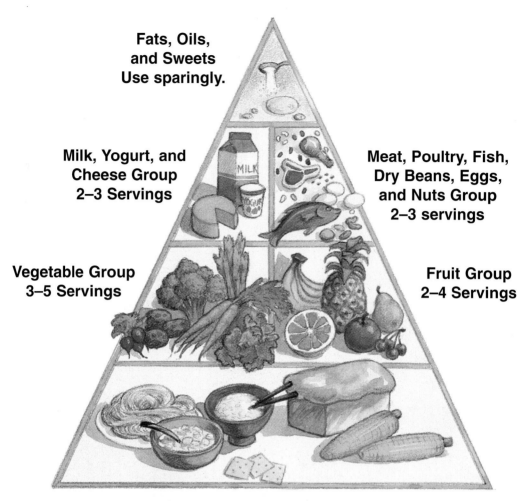

**Fats, Oils, and Sweets
Use sparingly.**

**Milk, Yogurt, and
Cheese Group
2–3 Servings**

**Meat, Poultry, Fish,
Dry Beans, Eggs,
and Nuts Group
2–3 servings**

**Vegetable Group
3–5 Servings**

**Fruit Group
2–4 Servings**

**Bread, Cereal, Rice and Pasta Group
6–11 Servings**

Another way to protect your body is to give it the best kind of fuel to run on. A balanced diet that includes many different foods helps your body work as well as it can.

You may already know that junk food doesn't provide enough nutrition. So, try to pick healthy choices from each of the major food groups. You may be surprised at how good these foods are and how much energy you have when you eat them. Remember, drink plenty of water, too!

Conditioning is another way to protect your body from injury. When you get your body used to physical activity, it will be ready to do whatever sport you want. Conditioning helps make your joints and muscles stronger and more flexible. This helps you become physically fit.

Conditioning usually includes stretching exercises for different parts of your body. Have you learned a set of exercises in gym class or at sports practice with a team? Continue doing these exercises during the summer to keep your body in good shape. You can also do exercises to strengthen the muscles and joints you use in a certain sport. However, if any kind of exercise causes you pain, stop doing it and tell an adult.

You should always warm up and stretch before you start to play. If you think about it, this makes a lot of sense. Warming up gets your heart and lungs to work faster. It makes blood flow to your muscles so they are ready to work hard. It's a great way to protect your whole body.

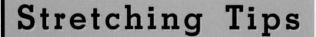

Stretching Tips

Spend about five minutes warming up.

Relax and breathe easily while stretching; don't bounce.

Do each stretch until you feel a slight pull in the muscles.

Hold each stretch for 5–10 seconds. Work up to holding for 20 seconds.

Do a stretch 3–5 times. Over time, increase to 10 times.

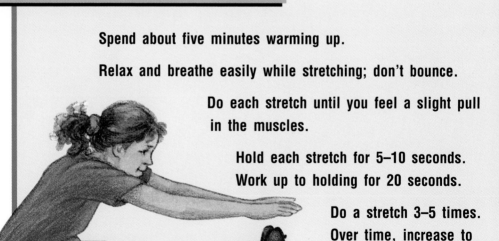

Warm-ups such as stretching help prevent your muscles from having cramps or spasms while you exercise. A spasm is a sudden painful tightening in a muscle. It may feel like a hard lump or knot.

A good warm-up takes at least 10 minutes. Perhaps you think taking time for a warm-up is a waste of time. You'd rather get right into playing your sport. Warm-ups are important and can be a lot of fun! Here are a few you can do.

Reach for Toes (Thigh-calf, lower-back stretch)

Sit with legs straight out, heels about 5 inches apart.

Slowly reach fingertips forward as far as you can go.

Ankle Pull (Front-thigh stretch)

Stand on your right leg.

Bend your left leg up behind you.

Grasp your left ankle with your left hand and pull gently.

Repeat, bending your right leg.

Experts say that after playing sports, you shouldn't lie down right away. Instead, you should "cool down." A cool-down helps keep your muscles from getting stiff, and it gives your heart a chance to slow down, too.

You may have seen professional athletes cooling down. After a race, runners don't stop and flop to the ground. They walk slowly around the track or along the grass. Walking is a good cool-down for any sport.

During your cool-down, do some stretches like the ones you did before you started playing. Stretching your muscles after you play helps keep you from feeling sore later.

Sidewalk and Playground Sports

Summer sports sometimes lead to cuts and bruises. This is especially true of "sidewalk sports," such as biking, in-line skating, and skateboarding. Any sport that's played on a hard surface can cause cuts, bruises, and blisters.

A cut is a break in your skin. Usually a cut bleeds, because blood vessels under the skin get broken, too.

A bruise is a dark area that forms on your skin after a hard bump. Small blood vessels, or capillaries, break under the skin.

A blister is a bubble-like swelling of the skin that is filled with watery body fluid. It is often caused by rubbing.

Cuts, bruises, and blisters hurt. Sometimes they hurt so much that you don't feel like playing anymore. If you do a couple of simple things, you can avoid getting them.

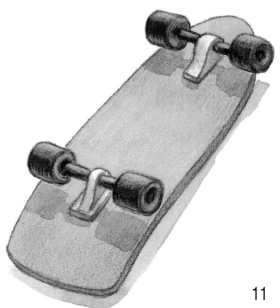

How to Avoid Cuts, Bruises, and Blisters

1. If it's not too hot, wear long pants to protect your legs.
2. Wear pads to protect your elbows, knees, and wrists.
3. Wear socks for any sport; this helps prevent blisters on your feet.
4. Wear gloves for long bike rides to protect your hands from blisters.
5. Use a clip or a rubber band to keep your pants from getting caught in your bike chain.
6. Make sure your shoes fit. Loose shoes can't grip a skateboard or bike pedals. Dangling shoelaces can get caught in wheels or under a foot.

Other kinds of equipment that protect you are a goalie's mask for street hockey, a batter's helmet for baseball, and shin guards for soccer.

It's no fun to watch all your friends playing sports while you wait for a sprained ankle or broken arm to heal. Some of the same equipment that prevents cuts and bruises can protect you from injuring a joint or breaking a bone.

1. For any sport that twists and bends your ankles, good support can help prevent sprains. Wear skates or shoes that support your ankles.

2. Wear pads that are designed for the sport you are playing. They provide protection and can help prevent injuries to joints and bones.

3. DON'T wear loose, floppy clothes or shoes. These can get caught and make you fall hard enough to sprain a joint or break a bone.

There's one easy way to protect your head while you play summer sports: **_Wear a helmet_.**

Why is a helmet so important when you bicycle, in-line skate, and skateboard? It's obvious. A fall can cause serious injuries to your head. Many biking injuries are head injuries. A helmet is designed to protect your skull and brain.

Some kids seem to think helmets aren't cool. Keep in mind, no professional bicycle racer would ever ride without one. Why would you?

Water Sports

Swimming is one of the most popular summer sports. It's fun and a great way to cool off in hot weather. It's also a great aerobic exercise that sends oxygen to your muscles. Try one half hour of steady swimming three or four times a week. This will help make your muscles, your lungs, and your heart stronger.

However, there is a danger all swimmers face—drowning. During drowning, water instead of air gets into a person's respiratory, or breathing, system. There is not enough oxygen reaching the person's brain. This causes death.

It's scary to think about drowning. Luckily, there are many ways to prevent it. Here are some simple suggestions for protecting yourself in the water.

1. Learn how to swim before you go into water deeper than your chest. Knowing how to swim makes you feel confident around deep water.

2. Never swim alone. Even if a lifeguard is on duty, he or she can't watch every swimmer all the time. Make a plan with a friend that you'll keep track of each other in the water. That way each of you will see if the other one is in trouble.

3. Never play rough in the water. It's too easy for someone to get pushed under for too long.

4. Never depend on an inflatable toy to keep you afloat in deep water. A tiny hole can make the toy lose air fast.

5. Never eat food or chew gum when you're in the water. It could make you cough or choke, and you could breathe in water.

6. Never dive unless you know how deep the water is and what rocks or other objects are under its surface.

The American Red Cross tells swimmers to watch out for the dangerous "toos." If you're too hot, too cold, too tired, too far from safety, or had too much Sun, you could have problems.

At first, being aware of these dangers may frighten you. However, learning about them will make you a more safety-conscious and better swimmer.

Boating is another popular water sport. Maybe you know how to use a canoe, a rowboat, or another kind of boat. When a boat has problems, people can drown. Knowing what to do before you get into a boat will keep you safe.

1 Learn to swim before going out in a boat.
2 Learn how to operate the kind of boat you are using before you take it out on the water. This includes knowing what to do if your boat takes in water or tips over.
3 Wear a life jacket.
4 Make sure someone knows where you are going and when you expect to be back.

Summer is a great time for activities you might not think of as sports. Many people like to hike in a park or woods. Do you enjoy camping in a forest or in the mountains? Maybe you go fishing at a peaceful lake far from town.

These are sports that many people love to do. The natural world is full of living things. Sometimes, they can cause problems.

Most people know what it's like to be bitten by a mosquito or stung by a bee. The bite itches or hurts and makes you feel uncomfortable.

It's hard to avoid getting bitten by insects, but you can try! Here's how:

1. Use insect repellent. Follow the directions on the label.
2. Don't wear perfume or anything sweet-smelling. It attracts insects.
3. Wear long sleeves and long pants so your skin is covered.

Usually an insect bite is not dangerous, and it heals fairly fast. But for some people, being stung by certain insects, especially bees, is very dangerous. These people are allergic to insect stings. They may have an allergic reaction that can cause death.

If you are allergic to insect stings, be sure to have your emergency kit ready whenever you are outdoors or away from home. Show your friends how to use it so they can help you in case of an emergency.

Ticks can also bite people. They are arachnids, along with scorpions, spiders, and mites. Some ticks are infected with serious diseases. It's important to protect yourself from tick bites. Experts give this advice:

1. Wear socks and shoes in areas where tall grass or trees grow.
2. Wear long sleeves and long pants. Pull your socks up over your pants.
3. Wear light-colored clothes so you can see dark-colored ticks that may fall onto you.
4. Check your skin and scalp for ticks when you go inside.
5. Use insect repellent that is made to keep ticks away. Follow directions on the label.

If a tick does bite you, it's important to see your doctor. Your doctor can help prevent a disease from developing.

Insects and ticks are not the only creatures that can bite people. Small wild animals, such as squirrels, rats, and raccoons, might bite, if they are scared. So might some dogs and cats.

A bite or scratch from an animal can be dangerous, because it can cause an infection. Some animals have a serious disease called rabies. They pass on the disease when they bite. If it is not treated, rabies may result in death. So, it's best not to get bitten by any kind of animal. How can you avoid animal bites?

1. Don't walk up to or try to pet ANY wild animal or any pet animal you don't know.
2. Don't put your hand or foot in any holes in the ground or in hollow logs where animals may live.
3. Don't tease animals. If an animal becomes scared, it may protect itself by biting.

poison oak

poison ivy

Did you know that some plants can make you itch as much as twenty mosquito bites? It's true! Certain plants, such as poison ivy and poison oak, cause an itchy rash on most people's skin. How can you protect yourself from these plants? Follow these two rules:

1. Learn to recognize the poisonous plants in your area. Then you can easily avoid them. Remember that some plants may change to their fall colors while you're still on summer vacation.
2. In the woods or other natural areas, walk on the paths or in open spaces.

Other plants can cause different problems for some people. Hay fever is one kind of allergic reaction to the pollen of some plants. Allergic reactions to plants include rashes, itching, red watery eyes, sniffling, and difficulty in breathing.

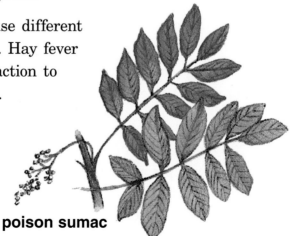

poison sumac

If you know you are allergic to some plants, you may be able to protect yourself from allergic reactions. Your doctor may give you pills or other medicine that will help. If you have trouble breathing, you may be able to use an inhaler that helps you stop wheezing.

The best way to protect yourself from summer plant allergies is to stay indoors until those plants stop blooming. That's not much fun, however. Talk to your doctor about other ways to prevent allergic reactions while you're outdoors in summer.

Many kids think that summer is the best time of the year. However, summer isn't much fun if you can't play the sports you love.

Here are two pieces of advice that will keep you safe all summer:

1. Know yourself. Don't push yourself to do things you're not ready for. Don't let friends push you to do things you're worried about.
2. Ask yourself this question: Would I do this in front of my parents? If you think the answer is "No," stop! What you are doing is probably not safe.

Remember that professional athletes put safety first. If they don't play safe, they may be sidelined with injuries. The same is true for you.

Play safe and have fun with summer sports!

Read Aloud Activities
for School and Home

Safety Posters Working in groups, think about a safety topic mentioned in the story and design a poster that could be used in a doctor's office, health clinic, school, or gym. Make your poster colorful and easy to read. Then, present your poster to the class with a brief description of it and why you chose the topic.

More Sports Safety Choose a sport that you enjoy. Think about how you could make your participation in that sport safer for yourself and others. With a friend, make a list of safety precautions that are followed in your sport from protective gear to rules and regulations. Add a few safety tips of your own to the list and incorporate them into the game when you participate in your sport.

Curriculum
College of Educ....... & Human Servic...
University of Michi....... .rbor

LEVELED
BOOKS
SCIENCE

McGraw-Hill School Division
A Division of The McGraw-Hill Companies

ISBN 0-02-27858_-_

9 780022 785819

5